ADVENTURE!

ADVENTURE!

A KID'S GUIDE TO THE NEW RIVER GORGE

R. BRYAN SIMON

Ourea Publishing

ADVENTURE! A Kid's Guide to the New River Gorge

Ourea Publishing, PO Box 405,Fayetteville, WV 25840

www.oureapublishing.com

ISBN: 978-1-7336232-4-7

1st Edition

Notices:

The author and the publisher have made every effort to ensure that the information included within this text is as accurate and up-to-date as possible. To the fullest extent of the law, neither the publisher or the author assume any liability for any personal injury and/or damage to persons or property, or death as a matter of products liability, negligence, or otherwise, or from any use or operations of any methods, products, instructions, or ideas contained in the material herein.

Risk is always a factor in outdoor adventure. A user assumes all risks associated with this guide including, without limitation, all risks associated with hiking, biking, rafting, and other outdoor pursuits.

Cover Illustration: Mark Quire, quiregraphics.com

Illustrations: Mark Quire, Lucy Rowe, lucindaroweart.com

Photos: Peilee Ren, Kristy Rodrigue, Wayne Simon, Molly Wolff, Jay Young

PRAISE FOR ADVENTURE!

We are nuts about this book!

SQUIRRELS OF THE NEW RIVER GORGE

Wise quackers flock to read ADVENTURE!

DUCKS OF SUMMERSVILLE LAKE

This book will keep you buzzzz-y as a bee!

QUEEN BEE OF THE NRG

To Deb, my wonderful partner in adventure. I could never imagine, on that day so long ago on Mt. Kilimanjaro, a life so happy and fulfilling as the one I share with you.

WELCOME TO THE NEW RIVER GORGE!

ADVENTURE AWAITS EVERY TRAVELER, young and old, here at the New River Gorge! There are over 80,000 acres of beautiful Appalachian forest and river habitat to explore and enjoy. The area is an outdoor lover's paradise with enough adventures to keep a person busy for a lifetime.

Unfortunately, we all have school to attend or jobs to do, so *ADVENTURE! A Kid's Guide to the New River Gorge* is designed so that you can maximize your fun while visiting. The next chapter will give you the low-down on all of the cool experiences you can have here and the remaining chapters go into more detail and include fun activities that you can do while exploring the New River Gorge. This adventure guide also includes fun activities that you can complete while gathered around the campfire or waiting for dinner! Always remember, be safe, listen to your parents and your guides, and above all else...have FUN!

PARENTS: In addition to the fun activities included in the book, you can find detailed directions on how to get to the different areas or trails mentioned within. You will also find lots of information regarding lodging, restaurants, and activities at the back of the book. Look for text in italics in each chapter for directions and other details!

Let's get started!

Cool off with a nice swim in Summersville Lake. © 2018 Jay Young, Courtesy of Adventures on the Gorge.

CHAPTER ONE
ADVENTURES ALL AROUND

ARE you ready to start your adventure packed visit to the New River Gorge? This chapter provides information about some of the most common and fun things to do here along with some tips to get you started. At the back of the book there is also an *ADVENTURE!* list that you can check off as you complete each activity!

CAMP

Camping is always fun in the New River Gorge and there are plenty of locations to pitch your tent and sleep under the stars! Roast marshmallows and make s'mores beside the campfire, watch lightning bugs light up, tell ghost stories, and search the skies for constellations like the Big Dipper. A list of campgrounds is included in the "Sleep Tight and don't let the bugs bite!" section.

CLIMB

The New River Gorge and surrounding area is home to around
3,500 different climbing routes! These climbs range from
pretty easy (5.4) to really, really hard (5.14c). So, whether you
are new to the sport or a superman climber like Alex Honnold,
there is something here for you. Don't have any experience and
no equipment? No Problem! There are two climbing focused
guide services in Fayetteville that can take care of you and
"show you the ropes!"

The New River Gorge, Meadow River, and Summersville
Lake have some of the best climbing in the US. © 2018
Molly Wolff, Molly Wolff Photography.

HIKE

Go for a hike, or two, or three! There are 48 trails in the New River Gorge ranging from easy to difficult and from short (0.11 mi.) to really long (8.34 mi.). In the "Trail Treasure Hunts!" and "Hidden History!" chapters you will find a number of fun hikes. There are also over 60 additional trails in nearby state parks. For more information on these hikes, check out *Hiking and Biking in the New River Gorge: A Trail User's Guide* (available in print and e-book) for a comprehensive listing of trails, difficulties, and historical and cultural notes on each.

You never know what you will find while hiking in the New River Gorge. © 2017 Wayne Simon.

DID YOU KNOW?

The New River Gorge has around 3,500 different rock climbs and 48 trails!

MOUNTAIN BIKE

The New River Gorge is one of a handful of national parks that allows mountain biking. Take advantage of it! There are a number of easy rail trails and some more challenging and technical single track for experienced riders. The Southside Trail (6.39 mi.) is relatively flat with a few rises. This trail features the remains of many coal towns and lots of wildlife. There is even a resident bobcat that is often seen by locals. Don't worry, he doesn't like to get close, but keep your eyes peeled!

For a true mountain bike experience, head over to the Arrowhead Trail System. This network of four trails was built by Boy Scouts and each path (Adena, Clovis, Dalton, and Lecroy) is named for types of arrowheads and spear points used by prehistoric Native American cultures who lived in this area. These trails are "stacked" so you can combine them in different ways. The Clovis trail is a good introduction to "actual" mountain biking in the region.

There are miles and miles of mountain bike trails in the New River Gorge. © 2018 Peilee Ren.

RAFT

The New River and the Gauley River have some of the best whitewater in the United States. The New River season runs from the spring to the fall. The Upper New River is a perfect trip for the first-timer and if you are six years or older you can experience the thrill of running rapids! The Lower New River is a little more intense and for older, more adventurous souls! You have to be at least 12 years old to run this portion of the river.

The New and Gauley Rivers have great whitewater!

The main season for the Gauley River is the fall when the rapids grow with the release of water from the Summersville Dam. People travel from all over the world to test themselves in the big rapids. There is also a summer season on this river, but the minimum age is usually 14 to 15. Other fun options include a trip down "the Dries" or a float on Glade Creek.

Laugh, scream, and look funny at your friends
while on the river! © 2018 Peilee Ren.

SKI, SNOWSHOE, AND SNOWBOARD

If you are visiting in the winter, many of the trails in the gorge
are suitable for cross-country skiing and snowshoeing. One of
the best times to explore is after a fresh snow as you can see
things that are normally hidden thanks to a blanket of the white
stuff. Some examples of items "hiding in plain sight" include:
old coal cars, walls and foundations of ghost towns, and even a
small stone building nestled into the side of the gorge! A snowy
hike is also a great time to identify animal tracks. Check out
Chapter 6: All the Animals BIG and small, for pictures of
common animal prints here in West Virginia.

If you enjoy downhill skiing, snowboarding, or snow tubing you
can travel just a short distance south to Winterplace Ski Resort.
There are 27 runs and a terrain park. They even have lights so
you can ski at night!

SEA KAYAK AND STAND UP PADDLEBOARD (SUP)

Summersville Lake is the best place to sea kayak or SUP. There are lots of places to explore and to launch you own personal "ship." A great adventure is to paddle to the island just off of Battle Run beach and explore. Another idea is to visit the waterfall at Pirates Cove! Who knows what treasure you might find!

Exploring Summersville Lake by SUP. © 2018 Jay Young, Courtesy of Adventures on the Gorge.

SWIM

One of the best places to go for a swim is Summersville Lake. There are a number of locations to go, such as Battle Run beach. Some spots even have large boulders you can swim out to if you want! Many local creeks also have beautiful swimming holes and Ace Adventure Resort, Adventures on the Gorge, and River Expeditions have swimming facilities.

Always remember to listen to your parents and lifeguards and to wear a personal flotation device!

DID YOU KNOW?

Summersville Lake is one of the clearest lakes east of the Mississippi River and is popular with scuba divers. There are even sunken boats on the lake bed for divers to explore!

Soar through the air like a super hero on a zip line! © 2014 Sterling Snyder, Courtesy of Adventures on the Gorge.

ZIP LINE

Want to be a super hero? Zip lining allows you to fly through the sky! Many local facilities offer zip lines. Combine a morning of zip lining with an afternoon canopy tour and you have an adventure filled day. Tree top tours are obstacle courses in the sky, lots of fun, and are highly recommended!

OTHER ACTIVITIES

These are just some of the amazing activities you can do while visiting the New River Gorge. There are also a number of indoor fun activities in case the weather is not cooperating! You can visit the museum in the Canyon Rim Visitor Center or the Boy Scouts of America Visitor Center (just south of Fayetteville on Rt. 19), check out the Exhibition Coal Mine and museum, go bowling at Pinheads, see if you can solve a puzzle in the Epic Escape Room, visit the Mystery Hole, or take a drive to see waterfalls (Chapter 8).

CHAPTER TWO
THE ONE HOUR
ADVENTURE WARM-UP

WANT TO GET STARTED? Well, let's go! This adventure begins at the National Park Service Canyon Rim visitor center at the New River Gorge bridge. Follow the directions included in this chapter and you can experience an hour (or more) of ADVENTURE right now!

PARENTS: The following section has a detailed plan and driving directions for a fun introduction to the area.

STOP 1: CANYON RIM VISITOR CENTER

Ask the ranger on duty about how to become a Junior Ranger (see Chapter 11 for more information). Make sure to check out the huge 3D map of the New River Gorge and the small museum. Before you leave, don't miss the museum and the animal poop display (it's fake and not stinky)! Turn to Chapter 6 to match the poo to the animal. Once you have done all that, head back to your car for the next stop!

STOP 2: HEAD UNDER THE BRIDGE

From the visitor center, take a right and drive along Lansing Loop road until you meet Fayette Station road. Make a sharp (!) right turn and follow Fayette Station (it is really curvy!) for 0.4 miles. When you get to the bridge, drive under it and park in one of the next two paved turn-outs. *When in doubt, always take the option to head downhill!*

STOP 3: THE NEW RIVER GORGE BRIDGE

Standing 876 feet above the river, the bridge was completed in 1978. Before then you had to use Fayette Station Road to get across the river. What a time saver! Walk back to the bridge and look underneath. You may hear voices, but don't be scared, it is just visitors walking under the bridge! Look carefully and you can see the scaffolding that they use to cross the gorge. Check out the activities section in the back of the book for more details on how you can take a tour under the bridge (Bridge Walk).

There are also a number of information boards that give details about the bridge and how it was built. Keep on the look-out for a groundhog. As of 2019, a friendly groundhog was living under the bridge and very near the road!

Stone stairs leading to the rope climb at Bridge Buttress.

STOP 4: ROPE CLIMB FOR THE BEST VIEW IN THE GORGE

From where you parked, head down the road (toward the river) for about 100 meters and watch for a trail on the right side of the road called Bridge Buttress Trail. Climb the stairs and head to the left of the massive rock in front of you. This is a very popular climbing area and you will likely see a number of climbers on the rock. Follow the wide path with the rock wall on your right. If you look closely, you might see white spots on the rock. These marks are from the chalk that climbers use to keep their hands dry.

After about 50 meters the trail curves right to a stone staircase. Climb these stairs and you will arrive at the rope climb. Pull yourself up hand-over-hand and once at the top, head to the right. Carefully walk along the trail until it opens up to a beautiful gorge view.

There is plenty of room to take in the view, but watch your step as you are near a 100-foot cliff!

STOP 5: FAYETTE STATION ROAD & THE TUNNEY HUNSACKER BRIDGE

Continue down this windy 100-year-old road that used to be the only way across the New River Gorge until you reach the Tunney Hunsacker (Fayette Station) Bridge. You might not realize it, but two towns once stood on either side of the bridge. Ask your parents to let out all the passengers and walk across the bridge (they can park on the other side). Watch for rafters and kayakers floating beneath your feet and don't forget to look up and see the higher bridge!

The Tunney Hunsacker Bridge is a favorite with visitors. © 2016 Peilee Ren.

View of the New River Gorge Bridge from the Tunney
Hunsaker Bridge far below.

STOP 6: FAYETTE STATION RAPIDS

Just past the bridge is a large parking area. Park here and head
to the beach. This is one of the best places to watch rafters
negotiate Fayette Station Rapids and also a great place to skip a
stone into the river! It is also the landing zone for B.A.S.E.
jumpers on Bridge Day.

STOP 7: WOLF CREEK AND KAYMOOR TRAIL WATERFALLS

Jump in the car and drive back up the gorge for one mile until
you reach the Kaymoor Trail trailhead. There is parking just
after the very deep bend in the road. Start down the Kaymoor
trail, using the steel bridge to cross Wolf Creek and head 200
meters to see Kaymoor Trail falls. This waterfall flows right

beside and under the trail and is a great way to cool off on a hot summer day.

Want to see another waterfall? Head back to the parking area and walk a short way down the road (toward the river). Watch to your right and you will be able to see the Wolf Creek Falls. There is a steep trail that leads to Wolf Creek just below the falls but it can be slippery, so be careful!

Kaymoor Trail Falls.

STOP 8: UP AND OUT OF THE GORGE

After jumping back into your car, wind your way back up the gorge. You will drive under the bridge again. Keep watching to your right and you will get to see another waterfall. This one is called Marr Branch Falls and is right beside the road! If you visit in May or June, you will even see rhododendron blooms surrounding the falls. A short distance later you will arrive at the top of the gorge. You can turn right onto Rt. 19 to head into Fayetteville or turn left to complete a loop across the New River Gorge Bridge and back to the visitor center!

CHAPTER THREE
TRAIL TREASURE HUNTS!

HIKING IS ALWAYS FUN, but it is even better when you are on the lookout for furry creatures and interesting objects! Two of the best trails for treasure hunting in the New River Gorge are included in this chapter. This area is filled with natural treasures just waiting to be found. But remember, the best treasures, once found, are left behind so the next young adventurer can find them too!

The key to any treasure hunting expedition is to have a good map. The maps included here will keep you on the trail and guide your path toward finding treasure! So, let's get started on our natural treasure hunting adventure!

THE ENDLESS WALL TRAIL

While the name makes you think the trail might never end, the hike is only 2.4 miles long and leads to a spot called Diamond Point. Sounds like treasure might be found there!

How to reach the trail (Show your parents!): From the Canyon

Rim Visitor Center, head north on Rt. 19 and make the next
right turn onto Lansing-Edmund Road. Continue 1.3 miles
until you see the Fern Creek parking area (on the right). If the
parking lot is full, do not park on the side of the road. This is a
busy road and you might get towed!

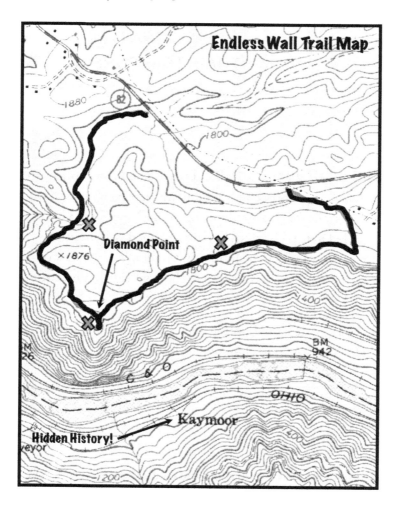

The trail begins in a forest thick with hemlock trees and rhododendrons. These trees make the area cooler than the

surrounding forest. Keep a sharp lookout for deer on either side of the path as they are often spotted here. Continue along the trail and you will begin to see mossy rocks and trees and keep your ears open for the sound of water!

The bridge across Fern Creek.

At 0.4 of a mile you will come to a stream. Cross the bridge and take a look into the water. Do you see any frogs or fish? Climb up the opposite side on large rocks. Hey, did you notice the trees changed? You just walked into a stand of oak trees! Can you find a leaf? See if you can identify it using the leaf identification illustrations in Chapter 7!

The trail begins to angle to the left and you might start to feel a breeze coming out of the gorge. Soon you will see a sign saying "Climber's Access." This side trail will take you to the Fern Creek Ladders. You can follow climbers into the gorge by using this path if you want to make a side trip. To reach the bottom of the cliff you must head down the hill, climb down a ladder, walk through a rock tunnel, and go down another ladder!

SAFETY TIP!

At this point, the trail parallels a steep cliff. Keep well away from the edge!

Once you are back on the trail, you will see many smaller paths branching off to the right. Careful! These little tracks lead to a cliff! Continue walking a little further and you will reach a larger side trail and a sign to Diamond Point. This is one of the most visited spots in the New River Gorge. Head down this trail to an overlook and you will reach a true "diamond in the rough!"

View of the New River Gorge Bridge from
Diamond Point.

From this spot, you can see one of the longest stretches of the New River Gorge. Keep your eyes peeled for climbers on the rock to either side and watch the rapids below for any rafts floating down the river. Enjoy the breeze while you are here.

Often you will see birds floating on the wind! (Never throw rocks off of the cliff! There are often climbers and hikers below!)

The view of Endless Wall from Diamond Point.

There was a fire along this trail in 2014 that scorched the area above and below the cliff. Can you find any trace? The forest has mostly recovered, but some trees still show burned areas near their trunks.

You now have a decision! Head back the way you came for a 2-mile journey, or continue exploring along the gorge rim? If you want to go for the shorter walk, take a left, but if you want more adventure, turn right! If you turn right, you will discover a number of other overlooks and two more signs pointing to ladders for entry into the gorge.

DID YOU KNOW?

Endless Wall Trail was named the "Best Trail in America" by *USA Today* in 2015!

Keep going past these signs and the trail curves left and into a rhododendron grove. Soon you will cross one last bridge and begin to climb to a parking area. This is the Nuttall parking area. To reach your car, turn left and walk beside the road to compete the full circle.

LONG POINT TRAIL

This trail takes you to one of the most unique spots to view the New River Gorge bridge. Bring snacks or a picnic lunch and enjoy a wide view of the surrounding country!

How to reach the trail (Show your parents!): From the Canyon Rim Visitor Center, head south on Rt. 19, cross the bridge, and continue to the first set of traffic lights. Turn left and drive through the town of Fayetteville. Continue for a total of 0.7 miles and turn left onto Gatewood Road. Follow the very curvy Gatewood road for 1.9 miles. At the top of a hill, turn left on Newton Road. Trailhead parking is available 50 meters on the left. Brown NPS signs also help guide the way!

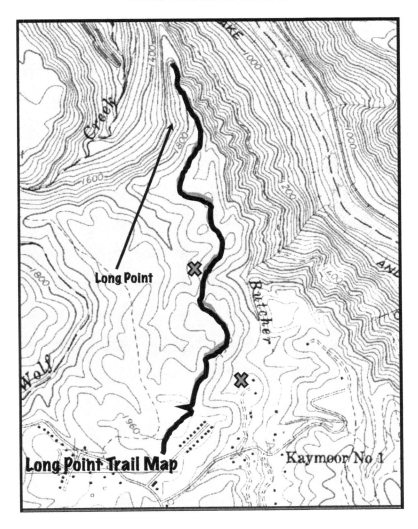

Long Point

Long Point Trail Map

Kaymoor No 1

The Timber Ridge Trail and Long Point Trail begin at this parking area. Don't accidentally take the wrong one! The Long Point Trail starts from near the toilet facilities. Also, remember to stay on the correct trail as Long Point intersects a number of other trails!

The trail begins in a small group of oaks and poplar trees and then breaks out onto a raised stone platform with a field on both sides. In the spring and summer, you can often see wildflowers blooming on both sides. At the end of this gravel walk there is a raised platform. In the evening, deer like to graze here.

View from the end of Long Point Trail.

Once you pass the platform, you re-enter the forest. There are many different types of trees here. Can you identify any of their leaves? Check out the leaf illustrations in Chapter 7 if you need help. As you wander through the forest, watch for squirrels — they love this trail. You will intersect the Fayetteville Trail and Butcher Branch Trail, but stay on Long Point. Soon the trail will begin to descend to one of the coolest features around... a rhododendron tunnel. The rhododendron bushes grow close and over the trail, creating a tunnel of leaves! Make your way through the tunnel and if you are visiting in May or early June, take a moment and smell the flowers. The rhodo-dendron flower is the West Virginia state flower.

Once you break out of the tunnel you will enter an area full of Virginia pine trees. Careful here, the trail is bordered on both sides by cliff! Continue down the trail and listen for the sounds of the Wolf Creek rapids below on the left. Soon the trees will open up to large flat boulders and a beautiful view of the New River Gorge and bridge! Relax, enjoy the view, and if you brought snacks, have a picnic! What treasures did you find on this trail?

WANT TO EXPLORE MORE TRAILS?

The Endless Wall and Long Point trails are just two of the 48 trails here in the New River Gorge. Looking to do some more exploring? Here are some other interesting trails to consider!

The "wash basin" tree on Big Branch Trail.

Polls Plateau Trail – This is one of the most remote trails in the national river and leads to an old homestead from the early 1900s. Look closely and you might find an ancient cooking stove with a porcelain front.

Big Branch Trail – This trail is found near the town of Hinton and is also very close to Brooks Falls and Sandstone Falls. Like Polls Branch, it is a little more difficult, but there are definitely some hidden natural treasures here. Follow the trail along Big Branch Creek and enjoy the waterfalls. At the top of the trail watch out for the "wash basin" tree off to the left of the trail!

CHAPTER FOUR
WHICH CAME FIRST?

THE PARK OR THE BRIDGE?

THAT IS A TRICK QUESTION — the river came first, and then the bridge, and finally, the park!

THE RIVER

The New River originates in western North Carolina and flows north through Virginia and West Virginia. It is 320 total miles in length and 53 of those miles run within the New River Gorge National River. The New River is actually thought to be part of an ancient river system called the Teays River that dates back to around 320 million years ago. The New ends when it connects to the Gauley River just northwest of the gorge and becomes the Kanawha River. The water that flows through the gorge eventually makes it way out of the mountains, into the Ohio River, and finally down the mighty Mississippi River to the Gulf of Mexico.

Everyone has fun in the water! © 2018 Kristy
Rodrigue.

THE BRIDGE

The bridge was completed on October 22, 1977. At the time of
its building, it was the largest single span bridge in the world. It
has since lost that title, but it is still one big bridge!

Can you imagine the gorge without the bridge? Some say it
took a 45-minute journey and turned it into a 45-second sprint!
While that is a bit of an exaggeration, the bridge has made life
more convenient for travelers and visitors to the park for
decades. The bridge took a little over three years to complete
and cost $37 million dollars.

To commemorate its construction, the area celebrates with an event called Bridge Day every third Saturday in October. The bridge is closed to traffic and it is the only day you can legally walk on the bridge. The day includes food and souvenir vendors, a running race, and B.A.S.E. jumping! For more cool facts about the bridge, check out the end of this chapter!

B.A.S.E. JUMPING

What is B.A.S.E. jumping? B.A.S.E. is an acronym for jumping from one of the following places: Building, Antenna, Span, or Earth. The New River Gorge National River is the only national park that allows B.A.S.E. jumping and you can only do it on Bridge Day. Jumpers from around the world travel here for the event. There is even a catapult that launches jumpers into the air! During this one day event, Fayetteville can grow from 3,000 people to nearly 100,000!

DID YOU KNOW?

The New River Gorge National River is the only national park that allows B.A.S.E jumping! But for only one day — the 3rd Saturday of every October. This is the famous Bridge Day when people from all over the world visit Fayetteville for the festivities!

Relaxing on the river. © 2018 Jay Young.

THE PARK

Just over a year after the completion of the bridge, President Jimmy Carter signed Public Law 95-625, creating the New River Gorge National River. The law allocated $20 million dollars to create the park and preserve 53 miles of river and over 70,000 acres of land. Since then, park rangers have protected the area's beauty and cultural heritage and opened these treasures to the public. If you see a ranger, thank them for their work!

MORE BRIDGE FACTS

- It lies 876 feet above the New River.
- It is 3,030 feet long.
- It cost $37 million dollars to build.
- It was the longest single arch bridge in the world (in 1977).

- It is now the third longest single arch bridge in the world.
- It is still the longest single arch bridge in the Western Hemisphere.
- It is the third highest bridge in the United States.
- It is the 13th highest bridge in the world.
- It weighs 88,000,000 pounds!

CHAPTER FIVE
HIDDEN HISTORY!

ANY GOOD EXPLORER likes to learn about the history of the place they are visiting. Here in the New River Gorge, we have tons of interesting historical locations. See Chapter 9 for more information on the ancient history of the region. This chapter takes you along trails and to locations of recent history with a focus on mining.

The industrial revolution and the discovery of coal hidden beneath the hills of West Virginia changed this area forever. Coal mining here began not long after the Civil War when the C&O Railroad completed tracks into the gorge in 1873. Millions of tons of coal were mined and numerous towns grew during this boom. Some towns, such as Kaymoor, Royal, Red Ash, and Nuttallburg no longer exist, while others, such as Thurmond (population: 5) are just hanging on. The trails included in this chapter will allow you to explore the ruins of some of these towns and see some of the creativity of their former residents.

Okay, budding archeologists, let's get going!

THE FACE TRAIL

How to reach the trail (Show your parents!): From the Canyon Rim Visitor Center, head north on Rt. 19 and make the next right turn onto Lansing-Edmund Road. Continue 0.3 miles and turn right on Fayette Station Road (CR 5/82). Travel 0.1 miles and stay left at a Y intersection and then continue 0.6 miles to a pull-off with an NPS information board that describes scenic drives in the region.

From the information board, walk 20 meters uphill along the road and watch for a trail that veers to the right. Take this path and follow it to a stone bridge. Look closely and you can see the name "Johnson" carved into one of the stones. After crossing the bridge, watch for the moss-covered face carved into the stone on the left of the trail. Take a moment to look at the detail.

Who carved this face? Legend has it that a coal miner named George Johnson carved a self-portrait into the boulder. He moved here in the early 1900s and is buried nearby in a local cemetery. If you continue down the trail you will also find a waterfall. From just above the waterfall you can cross the stream and head back to your car using a steep uphill trail or you can back track and check out George Johnson's stone carving one more time!

Who carved this face?

NUTTALLBURG AND SELDOM SEEN TRAIL

How to reach the trail (Show your parents!): This area takes a little while to reach, but it contains oodles of history! From the Canyon Rim Visitor Center, head north on Rt. 19 and make the next right turn onto Lansing-Edmund Road. Continue down this road for 6 miles. It progressively becomes curvier as you go along with a pothole or two! After 6 miles turn right on Keeney's Creek Road. This road is narrow but extremely pretty with a number of cascades along the route. The road ends at a parking area for Nuttallburg.

Some of the mine ruins in Nuttallburg.

Nuttallburg was founded in 1870 by, you guessed it, John
Nuttall. This area has some of the best-preserved ruins in the
New River Gorge. If you visit the Head house trail (more
details later), you will also see the mine that delivered coal to
the railhead here. If you look closely, you will find trees
growing between the old tracks! Another interesting historical
fact about the mine is that Henry Ford (Ford Motor Company)
briefly owned it and used the coal to power his automobile
factories in Michigan!

There are a number of trails that run through the ruins of the
mining complex and town of Nuttallburg. One of the best is
the trail to Seldom Seen.

The covered conveyor belt that brought coal to the train tipple.

Seldom Seen is the name of a town that was located just down river of Nuttallburg. Follow the Tipple Trail for 0.3 miles to reach the trailhead. The trail wanders through the forest for 0.25 miles to the ruins of the town. Here you will see the foundations of the homes that made up this town. You will also see a number of artifacts on the ground throughout the area. These include antique bottles, wash basins, and other items. Please leave all artifacts where they are so that other young explorers can find them too! These items, along with the ruins that surround them, are part of our cultural heritage!

KAYMOOR MINER'S TRAIL

How to reach the trail (Show your parents!): From the Canyon Rim Visitor Center, head south on Rt. 19, cross the bridge, and

*continue to the first set of traffic lights. Turn left and drive
through the town of Fayetteville. Bear left on Gatewood Road
and drive for two miles until you reach Kaymoor No. 1 Road.
Turn left onto this road and drive 0.9 miles until the road comes
to a T intersection. Turn left to the parking area.*

"Your family wants you to work safely."

The trail begins just prior to the parking area on the gorge side
of the road. This is a steep trail and requires some physical
fitness so be prepared! Hike into the gorge for one-half of a mile
to the main Kaymoor mine. You will know you have reached it
when you see the steel beam suspended in the air that says,
"Your family wants you to work safely." Visit the building and
ruins here including the No. 1 Kaymoor Mine and enjoy the
cool breeze coming from the entrance.

Once you have explored the area, you can continue to the bottom of the gorge using the wooden stairs. There are 820 stairs to the bottom and while going down is easy, coming back up is an adventure that will get your heart pounding! If you do take on this extra effort, make sure to look for railroad tracks on the side of the stairs.

It's a long way down... and up!

Railroad tracks? How did they do that? These rail lines were used along with a cable system to transport 15 miners at a time up and down the gorge. Mining was a dangerous job and even getting to work could be an adventure!

At the bottom of the stairs you will find ruins of the mine tipple and other buildings. There are a number of small trails here and the area can be rough to walk through. Be careful!

Mine ruins at the bottom of the stairs.

HEAD HOUSE TRAIL

How to reach the trail (Show your parents!): From the Canyon Rim Visitor Center, head north on Rt. 19 and make the next right turn onto Lansing-Edmund Road. Continue 2.5 miles and turn right onto Beauty Mountain Road. Travel 0.1 miles and park below the Nuttall Cemetery sign (at the 3-way intersection). As of April 2019, the National Park Service (NPS) is building an additional parking area here.

At the 3-way intersection, take the middle fork (the one that goes straight) and walk 0.15 miles to the trailhead. Continue into the gorge and after a little way down the path you will see boulders on your right and you might even see climbers working their way up the cliffs here! Continue to follow the trail as it zig-zags down the mountain. You will see another large boulder that looks like the front of a ship looming over the trail. A few more turns will get you to the Nuttall Head house and mine entrance!

The mine entrance at the Head house Trail.

This mine was open from 1873 until 1958. Miners would bring coal from the mine and dump it onto a conveyor belt that would transport it to the bottom of the gorge and onto rail cars. Take your time and explore the area. If you visit in the summer, enjoy the cool breeze that blows from the mine. It is nature's air conditioner!

Consider visiting Nuttallburg to see where the coal on this conveyor was loaded onto train cars.

CHAPTER SIX
ALL THE ANIMALS BIG AND SMALL

THE NEW RIVER Gorge is home to over 350 different animal species! They range in size from the large black bear to the tiny salamander. How many will you see on your visit? Let's take a look at the what you might run into while wandering the wild West Virginia woods!

The illustrations in this section can be colored with crayons or pencils. A great game to play is to color all of the animals that you see on your visit. Keep your eyes open, and when you see one, pay attention to their colors so you can complete the drawing as accurately as possible!

MAMMALS

The most common mammals in the gorge are white-tailed deer, gray squirrels, and chipmunks. But you never know what you might see! Black bears live here, as do skunks, raccoons, ground-hogs, bobcats, coyotes and red foxes to name just a few. River animals include muskrats, beaver, river otter, and mink. Smaller mammals include moles, shrews, and mice.

BLACK BEARS

The black bear is the state animal of West Virginia and are not only found here, but throughout North America. Though they may be called black bears, their shaggy fur can be blue/gray, blue/black, and brown. Black bears mostly eat grasses, herbs, and fruit, but they will eat other things they find, including fish and your camp food if you leave it out!

Black bears are very skillful forest residents. They can climb trees, run fast (24 miles per hour), and have a great sense of smell. Bears in the New River Gorge love blackberries, so if you are visiting in July, when the berries are ripe, watch for bears in berry patches!

BEAVER

Did you know beavers are the second largest rodent on Earth! Beavers do live here in the New River Gorge and neighboring areas and if you are near a river or stream, watch along the banks for stumps of small trees that have marks from their very big front teeth!

Beavers have all kinds of cool facial features! They have transparent eyelids that act as goggles when they swim underwater and their nose and ears have valves that close so they don't get any water in them! Of course, they also have enormous front teeth that allow them to eat all kinds of plants and trees. Some of their favorites are poplar, birch, maple, and willow.

Beavers can also become surprisingly large (30-60 pounds) and make quite a loud sound when they jump into the water. Great places to see a beaver is on the Southside Trail or at the Meadow River.

BOBCAT

Bobcats are the most common wild cat in the United States with estimates ranging from 750,000 – 1,000,000 in the country. They are elusive and hunt mainly at night, so while there are a lot of cats, humans don't often see them.

Bobcats are great hunters. They have fantastic night vision, can run at speeds up to 30 miles per hour, and are good swimmers. They can leap up to 12 feet in one bound and can climb well. Bobcats only eat meat and have very sharp teeth. Their diet includes rabbits, squirrels, mice, birds, and sometimes deer.

Bobcats have a very distinct spotted fur pattern though the color of their coats can vary and include: light gray, yellow-brown, brown, and red-brown. They also have a very distinct short, or "bobbed" tail, unlike a house cat or a mountain lion. There are plenty of these cats roaming the gorge and if you see one you will be very lucky!

COYOTE

Coyotes are very adaptable. At one time, coyotes were only found in the prairies and deserts of the western United States, but because they can easily adjust to a new area and new food sources, they are now common in the mountains of West Virginia. Like the bobcat, coyotes are nocturnal (night-time) animals. They are carnivorous (meat-eaters) and eat small mammals like rabbits, squirrels, and mice but will eat almost anything, including garbage, if necessary for survival. They can run up to 40 miles per hour and jump up to 12 feet. Unlike wolves, coyotes tend to hunt by themselves or in small families.

Coyotes look much like normal dogs and their fur colors range from gray-brown to tan-brown. They have a white throat and belly and their ears are pointy and stand up. Their tail is half as long as their body, and the end of a coyote's tail is black while the tip of a red fox's tail is white.

FOX

There are two types of foxes in West Virginia: the red fox and the gray fox. The red fox is much more common. Foxes, like coyotes, hunt by themselves rather than in packs like wolves. As with bobcats and coyotes, foxes are shy and elusive. They have exceptional hearing, great eyesight, and a good sense of smell.

Foxes hunt and eat small animals such as rabbits, mice, moles and squirrels. They also eat plants, and depending on the time of the year, eggs, fish, birds, fruit, and even garbage. Foxes will bury extra food to save it for later, a kind of "doggy bag!"

Foxes can travel great distances. They generally range up to four miles around their den site, but young males have been tracked to over 150 miles from where they were born!

OPOSSUM

Did you know that the New River Gorge has a marsupial living here? It is the opossum, also sometimes known as a "possum." Most marsupials, like the koala and the kangaroo, live in

Australia, but the opossum is common across the United States. Just like it's Australian relatives, opossums carry their newborns (up to 25 at a time!) in the mother's pouch for two months and then the babies get to ride on their mother's back for another month.

Opossums are about the size of a house cat and are grey in color. They have a prehensile tail that allows them to hang from branches and acts like a fifth hand. Opossums are nocturnal, meaning they look for food at night (put your camp food away!) and sleep in hollow logs, rock crevices, or burrows.

RABBIT

The eastern cottontail rabbit can be found in and around the New River Gorge, especially in fields and meadows that are common to the area. Rabbit fur is reddish-brown with lower areas being white. They are pretty small and weigh around three pounds. Male rabbits are called "bucks," females are called "does," and baby rabbits are called "kits." Rabbits have lots of predators. Some estimate that rabbits make up 75% of bobcat's diets and other predators include foxes, coyotes, dogs, cats, owls, hawks, and eagles.

RACCOON

Raccoons are nocturnal animals and don't be surprised if you see one out while camping! Raccoons have a very distinctive black mask across their eyes that make them look like bank robbers...they won't steal your money, but if you leave food out at your campsite, they might steal your leftovers! They also have a furry tail with black rings around it.

Raccoons eat both plants and animals and common foods include nuts, berries, insects, frogs, fish, and bird eggs. They will also eat food and scraps from trash bins. If your garbage bag is torn while you sleep, the culprit is almost always a raccoon!

Raccoons are agile and can climb trees well. They can sleep in trees, but they most commonly sleep in dens located in downed tree tops or rotten logs. They also can live a long time with some raccoons in the wild living up to 16 years, while those in captivity have been known to live for over 20 years!

SQUIRRELS

Squirrels are found throughout West Virginia and come in two varieties: the gray squirrel and the fox squirrel. They are considered rodents and like mice and rats, their teeth grow throughout their lifetime. While squirrels eat mainly nuts and seeds, they do also eat insects, fruit, snails, and bird eggs. In fact, most squirrels eat about a pound of food each week!

How do squirrels find their buried nuts? They have a fantastic sense of smell and it is estimated that they find 80% of what they bury... the rest become trees! Squirrels also have big eyes to help climb trees and protect them from predators like the red-tailed hawk.

Squirrels are very vocal and you can often hear them "barking." Barking or "chucking" along with two different types of tail movements are the way squirrels warn each other about potential danger!

But don't mistake them for these little guys! Chipmunks are smaller than squirrels and have light and dark brown stripes!

WHITE-TAILED DEER

After squirrels, white-tailed deer are the next most likely animal that you will see during your visit to the New River Gorge. They are the smallest deer in North America and are named after the white patch of fur that grows under their short tails. Males are known as "bucks" and female deer are called "does." White-tails have reddish-brown fur in the summer that dulls to a grayish-brown in the winter. Baby deer, called fawns, have the same color fur, but with white spots when they are young.

Male white-tailed deer grow a new set of antlers each spring and summer. These antlers fall off each winter. If you are really lucky, you might be able to find antlers during one of your trail hikes! White-tails are also very agile and can run through a thick forest at speeds of 30 miles per hour.

White-tailed deer eat mainly in the morning and evening. In the summer, most deer are solitary, except for female deer with fawns. In the fall, they tend to travel more in small herds of four to eight deer. Deer eat a variety of vegetation.

DID YOU KNOW?

There are 65 species of mammals, 233 species of birds, 48 different species of amphibian, and 38 species of reptiles that live in the New River Gorge!

WE ALMOST FORGOT... BATS!!

Bats live in the New River Gorge too! There are many abandoned coal mines that are ideal habitat for bats. There are ten different bat species that live in the area and two of those are on the national endangered species list. They are the Virginia big-eared bat and Indiana bat.

BIRDS

Hundreds of different bird species live here or migrate through the area and this includes 13 different types of birds of prey. Wild turkeys are abundant, and if you are lucky, you might even see a bald eagle or a peregrine falcon! This area is a true bird lover's paradise and hosts a bird watching festival every spring. You can learn more at: www.birding-wv.com.

If you are interested in birds of prey, check out the Three Rivers Avian Center (www.tracwv.org) for more information about educational programs and rehabilitation of injured birds in the area. The birds included in this section are just a small sampling of the 233 species that call this area home!

Ruby-throated hummingbird

BALD EAGLE

The bald eagle became a symbol of the United States on June 20, 1782 when it was designated as our national bird. Did you know that the bald eagle was almost extinct? The Bald and Golden Eagle Protection Act, originally passed in 1940 and then updated in 1962 and 1972, helped to turn the tide and biologists now estimate that there are almost 10,000 nesting pairs of bald eagles in the United States today.

Every spring a group of volunteers participate in an eagle
survey. In 2019, 35 different eagles were identified in the New
River Gorge! In fact, there is a well-known bald eagle nest on
the northern end of Brooks Island (near Hinton).

NORTHERN CARDINAL

The northern cardinal is the state bird of West Virginia (and six
other states) and is one of America's favorite birds! Most people
recognize the bright red male cardinal with his black face mask,
but miss his female companion. Female cardinals are pale
brown with hints of red. Both have very bright orange beaks.
You can see cardinals here year-round.

AMERICAN CROW

The American crow is a very noisy bird! Crows have black feathers that are shiny and have brown eyes. They are sometimes mistaken for a raven, but crows are generally smaller. Crows are also one of the most intelligent animals in the world! Scientists have observed crows using tools, storing food, and using bread crumbs as fishing.

DID YOU KNOW?

Crows eat a wide range of things including fruit, nuts, insects and even small animals such as frogs!

RED-TAILED HAWK

The red-tailed hawk is one of the top predators in the area. They silently hunt while flying or perched on high branches in the forest. Their feathers are generally brown with white and black mixed in and one type have brick red tails. Their breast is tannish-white in color.

(While writing this book, a red-tailed hawk visited me almost every day, perching on a branch just outside my office window on the lookout for mice and chipmunks!)

AMERICAN ROBIN

The American robin is the most common bird to see in the area, and if you are camping, you might see one rummaging around your campsite in the morning when you wake up! They are most easily identified on the ground as they run, hop, and peck for earthworms. Robins have a brick red chest, gray back, and streaks of black on a white chin.

Robin nests are made of twigs and mud with dry grass on the inside. Sometimes the nest will include bits of string or ribbon. Their nests are usually built in a bush, tree, or under the eaves of buildings.

WILD TURKEY

Did you know that Benjamin Franklin wanted the wild turkey to be named our national bird instead of the bald eagle? There are a lot of turkeys here in the New River Gorge and it is not uncommon to see a mother turkey with her babies poking around. And while we are talking about babies, did you know that they are not called "chicks" but instead "poults?"

Male and female turkeys definitely look different! A male turkey has a bald red head and a beard that can grow to be nine inches long! Males also are more colorful with feathers that have shades of green, gold, red, and purple, while females have generally brown-gray feathers.

While they look kind of awkward, turkeys are actually very fast! They can run up to 25 miles an hour for short stretches and can fly at 55 miles an hour! They need this speed as turkeys have many predators in the forest including bobcats, foxes, coyotes, eagles, and owls!

WOODPECKERS

There are nine different wood-peckers that call the forests of the New River Gorge home. If you hear a fast "knock, knock, knock, knock," while roaming the woods, it is likely one of these wood-peckers searching for insects by repeatedly driving their hard beaks into the bark of a tree.

Woodpeckers come in various shapes and sizes, but all of the ones that live here are red, black, white, and brown in color. The largest woodpecker is the pileated woodpecker. These woodpeckers were scarce at one time, but have rebounded and are easy to see in the forest due to their size!

A little-known fact about wood-peckers — they have feathers that cover their noses. These feathers catch all of the "sawdust" that they create by banging away at trees and keeps them from inhaling the dust! They also have four toes on each foot — two in front and two in back. This helps them to hang onto trees and branches more easily!

REPTILES AND AMPHIBIANS

There are over 40 different species of reptiles and over 50 different species of amphibians that live in the New River Gorge. In fact, West Virginia is home to one of the most diverse populations of salamanders in the United States, with over 34 different species. More than any other state!

Two poisonous snakes live here: the copperhead and the timber rattlesnake. Both are shy and you will likely not see one, but if you do, keep well away from them! Remember, snakes are cold-blooded and will search for warm places to lay, especially after cool spring or fall nights. They commonly sun themselves on rocks. If you or someone in your group is bitten, stay calm, and slowly walk back to your car. Most hospitals in the area have antivenin (a medication to counteract the poison)!

COPPERHEAD SNAKE

Copperhead snakes are venomous and live in 28 states. They have reddish-brown bodies with a cross-band pattern of tan, copper, and brown colors along the length of their body that look light hourglasses. Other snakes look similar to the copper-head and include the northern water snake, eastern rat snake, and eastern milk snake.

Copperhead snake

TIMBER RATTLESNAKE

The timber rattlesnake is not as common here as the copper-head. They can get up to 60 inches long and weigh almost ten pounds! They eat small mammals, frogs, birds, and sometimes, other snakes.

TURTLES, FROGS, AND SALAMANDERS

There are a number of different types of amphibians in the New River Gorge. If you are truly lucky, you will see a giant salamander that is native to the area called a hellbender. They can grow to be over two feet long!

ANIMAL TRACK ID GAME

One of the best outdoor games that you can play is the animal track identification game! This game is great anytime, but best after a rain or snowstorm when you can more easily see the tracks that animals left behind! Looking for prints in the mud that surrounds a water puddle or on the sandy bank of a stream are good places too!

You might not get to see a bear while you are here, but you are much more likely to see a paw print! The prints included here are for some of the most common animals in southern West Virginia. Good luck and happy hunting!

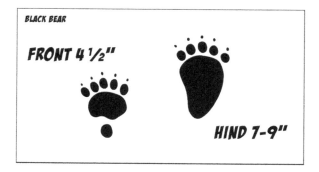

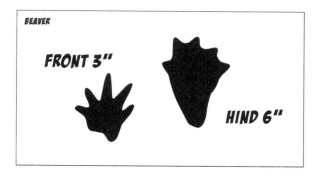

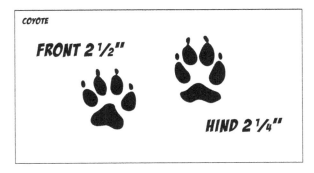

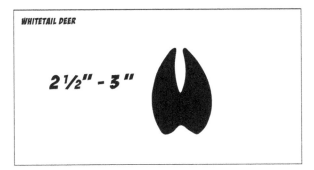

Use this space to keep track of how many tracks you can find!

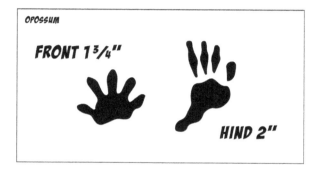

Use this space to keep track of how many tracks you can find!

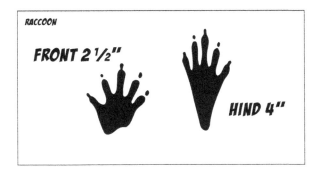

Use this space to keep track of how many tracks you can find!

CHAPTER SEVEN
TREE TIME

DIVERSITY BEST DESCRIBES the trees and plants of the New River Gorge. There are well over 1,800 different species of plants within the national river and surrounding state parks and entire books have been written about the different plants, flowers, and trees in this region.

The forest of the New River Gorge is considered mixed mesophytic. What is that? What that means is that the forest receives a moderate amount of moisture, though if you ask locals, they will probably say the area receives a lot of moisture in the form of rain! There is a mixture of deciduous (hardwood) trees as well as coniferous (evergreen) trees. We will get into more detail on what those words mean in just a moment!

West Virginia has over 100 different tree species. But there is one tree you will not see while here in the New River, and that is the American chestnut. The chestnut was once the most common tree to the region, but a disease (chestnut blight), wiped it out in the early 20th century. You can see old logs of chestnut if you visit one of the cabins built in 1937 by the

Civilian Conservation Corps (CCC) located at Babcock State Park.

DECIDUOUS TREES

Deciduous trees lose their leaves once a year in the fall after changing color from vivid green to shades of red, orange, and yellow. One of the prettiest times of year in the New River Gorge is late October when all of the leaves are changing colors! Examples of deciduous trees include: oak, hickory, ash, and elm.

CONIFEROUS TREES

Coniferous trees have needles instead of leaves. They don't change color, and their needles do not fall off like the leaves of deciduous trees. Coniferous trees, also commonly known as "evergreens," spread their seeds through the cones (cone-ifer-ous!) they produce and remain green throughout the year. Examples of coniferous trees include: pines, hemlocks, and spruce.

LEAF IDENTIFICATION - THE LEAF ID GAME!

A very fun activity while camping or going for a hike is to iden-tify the leaves of trees that tower above! You can play the Leaf ID game by yourself or with friends. Who can find and identify the most? The great thing about this game is that you can play it every time you go for a hike or anytime you go camping.

The rules are simple. Set a time limit, perhaps 15 minutes, and start collecting! The trees listed in this section are 21 of the most common here in the New River Gorge. With each leaf illustration, there is also a description of the tree and some interesting facts. Not only do you get to play a game, but you also get to learn about each tree! Remember, pick up leaves from the ground, rather than pulling them from the trees!

COMMON TREES OF THE NEW RIVER GORGE

ASH

Types of ash trees can be found in North America, Europe, and Asia. Their leaves turn yellow, orange, and red in the fall. Wood from the ash tree is often used to make baseball bats, hockey sticks, canoe paddles, and even musical instruments like drums and electric guitars!

The ash tree in the area is threatened by the emerald ash borer beetle. You may see triangular green or purple traps hanging in the trees. These are used to capture this beetle. Help keep the ash borer controlled, please do not transport firewood into or out of this area!

ASH

BEECH

There are 11 different types of beech trees and they can grow to be up to 100 feet tall. You don't see beech trees very often in big cities as they cannot live in air that contains large amounts of carbon monoxide (due to vehicle exhaust from burning gasoline). Beech wood is used to make furniture, floors for homes, and plywood.

BIRCH

There are over 60 different species of birch trees. They can grow to be up to 50 feet in height and their seeds and bark are eaten by birds, deer, and rabbits. Birch wood is great for campfires as it burns very easily. It is also used to build furniture, doors, and for the floors of basketball courts!

ELM

The elm tree used to be much more common, but an infection, called the Dutch elm disease, killed millions of the trees. In the middle ages, the elm tree was used to create longbows and the Native Americans used elm wood to build canoes. Today it is used for flooring and furniture.

HEMLOCK

Hemlocks can grow to be almost 200 feet tall, but in the New River Gorge, they usually are between 20 to 60 feet tall. They are threatened by an insect

BEECH

BIRCH

ELM

called the woolly adelgid which has killed a number of trees in the area. Animals and birds like to eat the bark, needles, and seed of a hemlock and you can often see birds relaxing on boughs of the tree!

HEMLOCK

HICKORY

The hickory tree can grow to be 100 feet tall and there are four main varieties: shagbark, shellbark, pignut, and bitternut. The nuts of a hickory tree are popular and squirrels are often found in a stand of these trees. Humans and deer like the taste of a hickory nut too! Hickory wood is used to smoke meat and for the manufacture of furniture, handles for tools, and paddles for canoes.

HICKORY

HOLLY

Be careful if you find a holly tree as the leaves have sharp ends! Holly trees stay green year-round. You often see holly branches around Christmas time as decorations and these trees have bright red berries. Don't eat the berries

HOLLY

though as they can cause vomiting and diarrhea!

BLACK LOCUST

This tree is native to central Appalachia and to the Ozark Mountains. Black locust leaves are 8 to 14 inches long and have 7 to 19 leaflets that connect to one small stem. They are found in North America, Europe, Africa, and Asia.

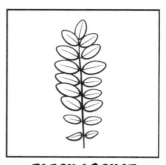

BLACK LOCUST

RED MAPLE

This tree's leaves turn a deep red in the fall and are one of the most beautiful trees during that time. The seeds of maple trees are also known as "whirlybirds" as they have a "wing" that makes a helicopter motion when they fall to the ground!

RED MAPLE

SUGAR MAPLE

The sugar maple is the state tree of West Virginia and the tree's leaf can be found on the national flag of Canada. The sugar maple also provides the popular sweet maple syrup for your waffles and pancakes!

SUGAR MAPLE

BLACK OAK

Oak trees make up 60% of all trees growing in West Virginia. There are 15 different types that can be found here, but the black oak is the largest and most common. It can grow to be 80 feet tall and its bark is rough and dark gray.

BLACK OAK

RED OAK

The red oak is very common and can grow to be 100 feet tall. Oak trees can produce up to 2,000 acorns in one year! That is good because acorns are loved by forest animals such as bear, deer, and squirrels.

RED OAK

WHITE OAK

White oak trees are the most valuable of oak trees. One of the largest oaks ever seen in West Virginia was found in Mingo County. It was 145 feet tall, the trunk measured over 27 feet in width, and it was estimated to be 582 years old when it died!

WHITE OAK

VIRGINIA PINE

The Virginia pine is the most common pine tree in West Virginia. It can grow almost anywhere and can reach 50 feet in height. You can find small groves of pines throughout the New River Gorge, but they are especially plentiful along the end of the Terry Top Trail.

VIRGINIA PINE

POPLAR

Depending on the type, a poplar tree can grow to be 165 feet in height! It also grows large roots systems that can almost reach as wide as it is tall! The wood of a poplar tree has been used to build snowboards and it is also used to create musical instruments such as guitars and drums.

POPLAR

RHODODENDRON

The rhododendron grows a beautiful pinkish purple flower that is the state flower of West Virginia. The New River Gorge hosts two types of rhododendron and if you visit in May and early June you might be able to see both in bloom. Rhododendrons do not

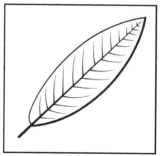

RHODODENDRON

grow to be very tall in this area and you will find them almost everywhere!

SPRUCE

There are three main types of spruce trees common in West Virginia. They are the red spruce, Norway spruce, and blue spruce. Their needles are similar in shape and the red spruce is the most common and only native spruce to the area. Spruce trees are used to make all types of musical instruments and the Wright brothers used it to build their first airplane!

SPRUCE

SWEETGUM

A sweetgum tree can grow to be 100 feet tall, but it is usually smaller in this area. Many forest creatures like the sweetgum seed, especially squirrels, cardinals, chipmunks, and blue jays. Native Americans used its sap as a type of chewing gum and the wood is now used in furniture making.

SWEETGUM

SYCAMORE

The American sycamore tree is commonly found near streams, rivers, and lakes. It can grow to be very large with heights up to 130 feet and trunks that measure over six feet in diameter!

They produce brown woody seed balls that measure one inch around and the wood of a sycamore is used for furniture, musical instruments, and cutting blocks.

WALNUT

Walnut trees produce the very popular walnut that is eaten by people around the world. Humans consume around 5 billion pounds a year and they are popular with animals too! Walnuts fall from the tree inside green husks that must be removed to get to the actual nut inside. If you find one in the forest it will take some effort to be rewarded with the delicious nut!

WILLOW

The black willow tree is native to West Virginia. It is usually found in swampy areas or along river-banks as it has a very shallow root system that requires constant moisture. Willow leaves turn yellow in autumn. Willow bark is used to produce aspirin.

SYCAMORE

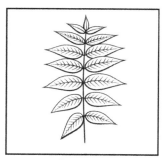

WALNUT

WILLOW

CHAPTER EIGHT
WILD WATERFALLS OF WEST VIRGINIA

WHERE THERE ARE MOUNTAINS, rivers, and streams you will almost always find waterfalls. In the area, there are three large rivers, the New, the Gauley, and the Meadow, and many large streams. Within each river and in most streams, there are also waterfalls. This chapter includes waterfalls of all shapes and sizes and directions on how to find them! Strap on your exploring shoes and get ready to see some wild water!

Waterfalling fun! © Eric Cain, Courtesy of
Adventures on the Gorge.

SANDSTONE AND BROOKS FALLS

While the New River is known for its whitewater rapids, the
river also has two large waterfalls located near Hinton, WV
where the river is wide and shallow. One is called Sandstone
Falls and the other is Brooks Falls.

*PARENTS: Sandstone and Brooks Falls are located on the
southern portion of the park and are best accessed from Inter-
state I-64. Use exit 139 and travel 14.1 miles on WV 20 to
Hinton, WV. Drive through this interesting railroad town and
cross the bridge before turning right onto WV 26. Brown
national park signs will help you find your way!*

This road travels along the New River. Keep your eyes open
and you will soon see Brooks Falls on the right! There is a
parking area here and this is one of the best places in the New
River Gorge to skip stones and have a picnic! If you have time
and want to see more waterfalls, the trailhead to the Big Branch

Trail is across the road. Read more about the hidden history of this trail in Chapter 5.

DID YOU KNOW?

The New River begins in North Carolina and flows north through Virginia and West Virginia! The New River is 320 miles long.

Sandstone Falls is a little further down this same road and is the largest waterfall on the New River. These falls are 1,500 feet wide with heights ranging from 10 – 25 feet! There are a number of hiking trails here that take you onto an island in the middle of the river. Take your time on these hikes and you will be rewarded with all kinds on surprises including smallmouth bass and other fish in clear pools and trickling falls all around the boardwalk.

Sandstone Falls is 1,500 feet wide!

WATERFALL ADVENTURE ROAD TRIP!

The waterfalls on this adventure road trip are easy to see and do not require any hiking! This is a perfect adventure if it is raining or if everyone is tired from hiking, biking, climbing, and other adventuring! From the Canyon Rim Visitor's Center travel south across the New River Gorge Bridge. At the first stoplight (Fayetteville), turn right onto WV Route 16 and drive (*Have your parents drive!*) five miles to a town called Beckwith. From here, the road will begin to drop steeply into the gorge with Laurel Creek on the left. Go slow here (!) and look over your shoulder as there are a number of waterfalls on this stream. There are no parking areas, so the slower you go, the longer you will get to see each of the falls!

Continue along the road, crossing the New River. Be sure to look right as you cross the bridge so you can see the Hawk's Nest Dam! This road will soon take you past another waterfall on the right called Big Creek before steeply climbing to an intersection. Stay left at the Y intersection and continue on the very curvy US Route 60. This intersection is known as Chimney Corner and there is a neat shop here.

Drive for 3.5 miles to the next waterfall called Cathedral Falls. This is one of the tallest waterfalls in the New River region and is 60 feet in height. The noise of the falling water echoes off the steep walls to each side and the roadside park is a nice spot for a picnic. You can dip your toes in the water here to cool off!

The last waterfall on this tour is Kanawha Falls. Continue west on US 60 and you will cross a bridge over the Gauley River. On your left, you can see some private islands in the middle of the New River with houses on them! This town is called Gauley Bridge and is at the intersection of the Gauley River and the New River. Once these two rivers flow together, they create the Kanawha River and the next waterfall is located in a town named Glen Ferris, WV.

Drive through Glen Ferris, home of the historic Glen Ferris Inn. This inn was established in 1839 and many famous people have spent the night here including four presidents (John Tyler, Andrew Jackson, Rutherford B. Hayes, and William McKinley). Continue past the inn and an electrical station and turn left into a park below the falls. This is the best place to view this very wide waterfall. You might see some kayakers or SUPers here and if you bring your own, you can get a closer look at the falls!

MILL CREEK FALLS AND FOX BRANCH FALLS

These waterfalls are most easily accessed from the lodge at Hawk's Nest State Park and includes a ride on an aerial tram all the way into the gorge! From the park lodge, take the tram to the river. Once there, pass the gift shop and restaurant and head to the Mill Creek Trail (Hawk's Nest Rail Trail). Hike this wide trail for 0.5 miles until you reach a wooden bridge. On your right, you will see Fox Branch Falls. Relax here for a moment and have a seat on the bench at the top of the falls!

Taking the aerial tram saves time and sore
muscles!

Once you have rested a moment, continue up the trail for 0.3
miles. Here you will find a side trail to the left. This side trail
takes you to the entrance of the Mill Creek Colliery Company
Mine. This mine dates back to 1921. A little farther up the
main Mill Creek trail you will also see the remains of a water
tower on the right. This tower once supplied water for coal
train's steam engines.

KAYMOOR TRAIL, WOLF CREEK, AND MARR BRANCH FALLS

These falls are included in Chapter 2 (The One Hour Adventure Warm-Up). Read more about them and all the surrounding adventures!

Kaymoor Trail Falls.

CHAPTER NINE
ANCIENT RESIDENTS OF THE GORGE

THE ANCESTORS of Native Americans came to the continent using a land bridge that connected present day Russia with Alaska. We know very little about these people, but eventually ancient Native Americans made their way to the New River Gorge. The first prehistoric native culture identified in this region were the Clovis people who lived here about 12,500 years ago. The only evidence of this culture are the Clovis spear points and stone tools found throughout the region. A trail in the park is named for these people!

The Adena people are the most closely associated with this area and populated the New River Gorge from about 800 BC to 1 AD. These Native Americans lived in a large region of the mid-atlantic and midwest including West Virginia, Ohio, Kentucky, and Indiana. The Adena were one of the first cultures that were hunter-gatherers as well as farmers. Some of the crops they planted include squash, gourds, sunflowers, and maize (corn).

An arrowhead collection of a local resident. ©
2015 Steve Hedgecock.

Archeologists have found Adena sites within the gorge. This
culture built mounds to bury important people and are often
referred to as "mound builders." These mounds can still be
found today. The largest identified is over 60 feet tall and 300
feet around! The Criel Mound in South Charleston, WV is the
closest mound to the New River Gorge.

The Hopewell Culture followed the Adena and lived in the
region from 1 AD to around 700 AD. These people were also
mound builders and lived in a much larger area and traded
extensively. The Hopewells also built defensive earthworks for
protection. Just west of the New River Gorge, along the
Kanawha River and near Mount Carbon, WV, railroad engi-
neers discovered an enormous rock wall measuring almost 10
miles long! We don't know why the wall was built. Was it for
protection? Did the Hopewell people use it for animals?

As you hike through the gorge, imagine what it was like here
12,000 years ago! Could you gather enough food to live? Could
you find a rock overhang to make into a home?

CHAPTER TEN
ALL ABOARD!

RAILROADS PLAYED a major role in the exploration and development of the New River Gorge. The railroad first came to the area in 1873 when the Chesapeake and Ohio (C&O) Railroad established its tracks. Trains were used to transport coal and timber from the area to factories around the country.

The Amtrak station in Thurmond, WV
(Population: 5).

Even today, trains continually run through the gorge heading east and west and transporting all types of material to cities across the United States. If you listen carefully, you will hear the train whistles throughout the day as they echo off the sides of the mountains!

A couple of future train conductors checking out the town of Thurmond. © 2018 Molly Wolff, Molly Wolff Photography.

The Amtrak system even has a passenger line through the area. The Cardinal line runs between Penn Station in New York City and Union Station in Chicago. There are three stops within the New River Gorge at Hinton, Prince, and Thurmond, WV. Today it is possible to travel by train from one of the smallest towns in America, Thurmond, WV (population: 5), to one of the largest cities in the United States, New York, NY (population: 8,600,000)!

DID YOU KNOW?

There are three Amtrak stops in the New River Gorge. Thurmond is one of the smallest Amtrak stops in the United States!

Many visitors ride a portion of this route in the fall to enjoy the changing colors of the leaves.

The National Park Service has a visitor center located in the historic Thurmond Depot. This restored depot will let you step back into time when this little town saw almost 100,000 visitors a year!

CHAPTER ELEVEN
BECOME A JUNIOR RANGER!

WHO WOULDN'T WANT to be a park ranger? These men and women get to spend every day in the New River Gorge and see all of the fantastic animals. Now you can also become a junior park ranger! Here is how:

1. Visit one of the four visitor centers in the area: Canyon Rim, Grandview, Sandstone, or the Thurmond Depot
2. Ask the ranger on duty for a Junior Ranger book
3. Do all of the activities listed in your book
4. Return your completed book to a Ranger
5. Receive your Junior Ranger badge and certificate

Congratulations! As a new Junior Ranger, share everything you learned with family and friends!

Extra **ADVENTURE!** Points. Do you like to fish? Now you can also earn the Junior Ranger Angler badge. Ask a Park Ranger for more details!

CHAPTER TWELVE
FAYETTEVILLE FUN

THE NATIONAL PARK is not the only place to have fun! There are many nearby state parks that also have fun activities and Fayetteville is full of fun shops and great places to eat!

FAYETTEVILLE

Did you know, Fayetteville is one of the "coolest" small towns in America? Yep, the town was given that award way back in 2006 by *Budget Travel* magazine. We have been keeping it cool ever since! After spending a day in the gorge, come to the downtown and check out one of the best outdoor shops in America, Water Stone Outdoors, and the many gift shops like Wild Art, Wonderful Things or the Great Googly Moogly!

Afterwards tour around our nifty downtown and get some dinner at any of our fab restaurants (Pies and Pints, Secret Sandwich Society, The Station, Big Dang Pizza, or the New River Curry House). Once you have had your fill, top it off with some ice cream from the Stache, try your luck at the Epic

Escape Room, or head over to the Fayetteville city park that
features a skate park, large playground, basketball courts, and
the trailhead for the Park Loop Trail.

The Historic Fayette County Courthouse with a statue of the
Marquis de Lafayette.

There is a lot to do in the area. Check out "Activities, Guides,
and Adventure Companies" to see all of the fun things you can
do while on vacation!

DID YOU KNOW?

Fayetteville, WV was named one of the "coolest" small
towns in the United States!

STATE PARKS, RECREATIONAL AREAS, AND A COAL MINE!

There are a number of state parks that surround the New River Gorge. Four of the closest are: Babcock State Park, Carnifex Ferry State Park, Hawks Nest State Park, and Summersville Lake Recreational Area. Each of these parks has a ton of fun things to do!

BABCOCK STATE PARK

Home to the historic Glade Creek Grist Mill, Babcock is a great place to fish, hike, and mountain bike. This park was created in 1937 by the Civilian Conservation Corps (CCC) and borders the New River Gorge. The grist mill is one of the most-photographed spots in West Virginia and is especially beautiful in the fall when the leaves are changing color.

The Glade Creek Grist Mill is one of the most photographed locations in West Virginia. (Babcock State Park)

CARNIFEX FERRY STATE PARK

Are you interested in the Civil War? This state park was the site of the battle of Carnifex Ferry on September 10, 1861. It is the best preserved Civil War battlefield in West Virginia. Union Brigadier General William S. Rosecrans attacked Confederate forces under the command of Brigadier General John B. Floyd. The Confederate forces retreated across the Gauley River.

HAWKS NEST STATE PARK

This park has some of the best views of the gorge. It also has an aerial tram that you can ride all the way to the New River and back again!

Train tracks at the bottom of the New River Gorge.

SUMMERSVILLE LAKE RECREATIONAL AREA

Located just 20 minutes north of the New River Gorge, Summersville Lake has tons of fun things to do! It is known as the clearest lake in the eastern United States. In fact, it is so clear you can even go scuba diving and see some sunken boats! You can hike, climb, SUP, or water ski here too. Don't miss Battle Run Beach for a refreshing swim!

There is a lighthouse located at Summersville Lake Retreat that allows a 360-degree view of the lake. It was built using a piece of a wind turbine tower and completed in 2009. Once you have spent the day swimming or SUPing at the lake, don't miss a stop at Fat Eddie's where you can pick up an ice cream, hot fudge sundae, or any number of cool treats!

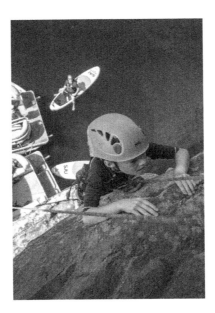

Swim, SUP, Climb, and explore at Summersville Lake! © 2018 Jay Young, Courtesy of Adventures on the Gorge.

EXHIBITION COAL MINE

The Exhibition Coal Mine, located just south of the New River Gorge in Beckley, WV, is a super fun way to learn about mining. Have you ever wanted to go into a mine? Now is your chance! Retired miners take you on a train deep into the mountain where you can learn how it is done, both in the past and today!

The museum has some fantastic exhibits and there are a number of buildings that are furnished as they were in the past. There is a playground, campground, and kid's museum too. It is a great trip to take on a hot summer's day or when the weather is not cooperating! For more information visit: www.beckley. org/general-information-coal-mine

THE GROWN-UP RESOURCE SECTION!

THE NEXT COUPLE of sections are for your parents, grand-parents, or whoever was cool enough to bring you to the New River Gorge! The information on the following pages will guide you to the best places to eat, sleep, and have fun while you are here! Read up on all the great fun you can have and point the highlights out to your parents.

Rappelling at Bridge Buttress. © 2018 Jay Young, Courtesy of Adventures on the Gorge.

ACTIVITIES, GUIDES, AND ADVENTURE COMPANIES

TELL YOUR PARENTS!

WANT to make the most of your visit and maximize fun? The list below includes local companies that offer all kinds of adventures!

ACE ADVENTURE RESORT

www.aceraft.com

Ace offers the following exciting activities: caving, climbing, disc golf, fishing, hiking, kayaking, obstacle course, paintball, rafting, rappelling, stand up paddle-boarding, and zip lines.

ADVENTURES ON THE GORGE

www.adventuresonthegorge.com

Adventures offers a ton of fun activities that include: caving, climbing, disc golf, fishing, hiking, horseback riding, kayaking, kid's camp, laser tag, obstacle course, mountain biking, paint-ball, rafting, rappelling, stand up paddle-boarding, a treetop canopy tour, and zip lines. Their facilities include various types of lodging, numerous restaurants, and a fantastic swimming pool overlooking the gorge. Enough adventure to fill days and days!

ARROWHEAD BIKE FARM

www.arrowheadbikefarm.com

Bike rentals and camping.

BECKLEY EXHIBITION COAL MINE

https://beckley.org/general-information-coal-mine/

Go deep underground and learn about mining history.

BRIDGE WALK

www.bridgewalk.com

Yes, you can walk across the gorge — under the bridge!

EPIC ESCAPE ROOM

www.epicescapegame.com/epic-location/new-river-gorge

Love a puzzle? Head downtown to think, solve, escape!

MOUNTAIN SURF PADDLE SPORTS

www.mtnsurfps.com

Stand up paddle boarding tours and rentals. Go get wet!

NEW AND GAULEY RIVER ADVENTURES

www.gauley.com

Boat, cave, climb, fish, hike, horseback ride, mountain bike and of course raft! Ask about their "mystery" tour.

NEW RIVER BIKES

www.newriverbikes.com

Mountain bike tours (along with sales and rentals) available with the friendliest guides around! Beginner to expert.

NEW RIVER CLIMBING SCHOOL

www.newriverclimbingschool.com

Climbing and rappelling for all ages and abilities!

NEW RIVER JET BOATS

www.newriverjetboats.com

Tour the gorge on a fast boat!

NEW RIVER MOUNTAIN GUIDES

www.newriverclimbing.com

Go "hang out" at the gorge! Rock climbing and rappelling instruction for beginners to experts!

PINHEADS

www.pinheadsbowling.com

Head to this awesome spot to bowl and have dinner!

RIVER EXPEDITIONS

www.raftinginfo.com

Offering ATV tours, canopy tours, climbing, fishing, hiking, horseback riding, mountain biking, paintball, rafting, rappelling, and zip-lining. Lots of lodging options and restaurants on site.

WATER STONE OUTDOORS

www.waterstoneoutdoors.com

The best, and friendliest gear shop on planet Earth!

WILD BLUE ADVENTURE COMPANY

www.wildblueadventurecompany.com

See the gorge from far above in a vintage biplane! Brave? How about some acrobatics!

SLEEP TIGHT

AND DON'T LET THE BUGS BITE!

THERE ARE all kinds of fun places to stay here and below are some of our favorites! Camping, glamping, cabins, hotels, motels, bed and breakfasts, and AirBnBs – we have them all in and around the gorge! Most places you can even make S'mores!

CAMPING & GLAMPING

This area is lucky to have a large selection on campgrounds to meet everyone's needs.

AMERICAN ALPINE CLUB CLIMBER'S CAMPGROUND

www.americanalpineclub.org/new-river-gorge-campground

40 sites with wooden platforms, shower house, No RVs ($8-$30)

ARROWHEAD BIKE FARM

www.arrowheadbikefarm.com

Small restaurant and beer garden on grounds, RVs ($8-40)

CHESTNUT CREEK CAMPGROUND

www.facebook.com/ChestnutCreekCampground

45 sites in the woods, quiet, shower house, No RVs ($10-11)

MOUNTAIN LAKE CAMPGROUND

www.mountainlakecampground.com

Family friendly with lots for kids to do. RVs and full hookups ($22 and up)

RAY'S CAMPGROUND

www.rayscampground.com

Family friendly, camping and cabins, RVs ($9-34)

SUMMERSVILLE LAKE RETREAT

http://summersvillelakeretreat.com

Camping, Cabins, and a LIGHTHOUSE! ($13.50 and up)

CABINS

There are a number of options for cabins in the woods. Check out these companies or consult listings on AirBnB.

ADVENTURES ON THE GORGE

www.adventuresonthegorge.com/lodging

Cabins of all shapes and sizes with many close to the gorge.

COUNTRY ROADS CABINS

www.wvcabins.com

Cabins galore and a new Treehouse!

MILL CREEK CABINS

www.millcreekcabins.com

Not far from the Endless Wall trail.

OPOSSUM CREEK RETREAT

www.opossumcreek.com

Great cabins in the woods.

HOTELS/MOTELS

There are not too many around town, but these two hotels are family friendly and have pools!

COMFORT INN

www.choicehotels.com/west-virginia/fayetteville/comfort-inn-hotels

QUALITY INN

www.choicehotels.com/west-virginia/fayetteville/quality-inn-hotels/wv401

BOUTIQUE INNS AND BED AND BREAKFAST

LAFAYETTE FLATS

www.lafayetteflats.com

Beautiful and wonderfully decorated vacation apartments in Fayetteville!

MORRIS HARVEY HOUSE

www.morrisharveyhouse.com

Traditional B&B.

AIRBNB

www.airbnb.com

As of printing, there are over 100 unique listings in the Fayetteville area

FUN FOOD SPOTS

PIZZA, BURGERS, ICE CREAM, AND MORE!

FAYETTEVILLE IS full of great places to eat to power up for a long day in the gorge or after a big day of adventuring! Show your parents and enjoy your favorite meal!

BIG DANG PIZZA

www.facebook.com/bigdampizza

Not the real name, but hey, this is a kid's book!

BURRITO BAR AT BREEZE HILL

www.theburritobarwv.com

Mexican with a view.

CATHEDRAL CAFÉ

www.facebook.com/cathedralcafe

Mmmm. Pancakes and lots more!

COUNTRY THAI

www.facebook.com/Country-Thai-Restaurant-WV-489790624436756/

Great curries!

FIRECREEK BBQ AND STEAKS

www.firecreekbbqandsteaks.com

Lots of barbeque!

NEW RIVER CURRY HOUSE

www.facebook.com/New-River-Curry-House-388459918379791/

Brand new for 2019.

PIES AND PINTS

www.piesandpints.net

Pies as in PIZZA! Pints as in for your PARENTS!

RANGE FINDER COFFEE

www.facebook.com/rangefindercoffee

Want to know the best way to get to visit Water Stone Outdoors? Tell your parents that they can get fair trade, specialty coffee right here!

SECRET SANDWICH SOCIETY

www.secretsandwichsociety.com

Shhh! It is supposed to be a secret... but the burgers, sandwiches, and fries here are really good!

THE STACHE

www.facebook.com/wvstache

Ice cream anyone? Fabulous flavors galore!

THE STATION

www.thestationwv.com/menu

Sit down and enjoy local sourced food. Did I mention peanut butter pie?

WOOD IRON EATERY

www.woodironeatery.com

Waffles! Sandwiches! Mom and Dad will love the coffee!

GROWN-UP FUN

There are a number of places for grown-ups too! Mom, dad, aunts, uncles, and grandparents might consider the following locations: The Grove, Southside Junction, Bridge Brew Works, Maggie's Pub and the Freefolk Brewery (new for 2019). Check out their Facebook pages and websites for more information.

ADVENTURE!
ACKNOWLEDGEMENTS

Thanks to all of my friends and family for their support on this project. The town of Fayetteville is a special place and I am lucky to call it home.

I especially want to thank my friend and long-time illustrator-extraordinaire, Mark Quire for his fantastic work on the cover and specialty illustrations. Special thanks to Lucinda Rowe for collaborating again with her expertly drawn animals and birds. Special thanks to Kristy Rodrigue, Molly Wolff, and Jay Young for allowing me to include their wonderful photography and thus share some of the special moments they have had with their children on adventures here in the New River Gorge.

Special thanks to all the kids that remind me as often as I allow them to that life is an adventure: Lia, Claire, and Annie Vander Kant; Jordan and Madison Vander Kant; Lucas and Siena Vander Kant, and Milo Smith.

Huge thanks to Peilee Ren for the photos, reviewing the text, and offering great advice and to Mark Pugeda for helping me write while in a cast and rehab my arm afterward!

And as always, I want to thank my wonderful wife, Deb. Your love, support, and encouragement makes all the difference and brings more happiness than I deserve!

ABOUT THE AUTHOR

R. Bryan Simon is a native of West Virginia. When not goofing off, adventuring, rock climbing, or hiking, he can be found at his house in the woods above the New River Gorge.

f facebook.com/rbryansimon

𝕏 twitter.com/rbryansimon

📷 instagram.com/rbryansimon

ALSO BY R. BRYAN SIMON

Hiking and Biking in the New River Gorge, A Trail User's Guide

Animals of the New River Gorge: Color and Learn

NEW RIVER GORGE
ADVENTURE CHECKLIST

KEEP track of all of your adventures right here! There is plenty of room to list all of the animals you see and trees you identify. Record the trails you hike or bike and make sure to put a star beside your favorite activity!

New River Gorge Adventure Checklist

- ☐ Take a hike
- ☐ Try out climbing
- ☐ Go rappelling
- ☐ Run a rapid in a raft
- ☐ Skip stones on the river or at the lake
- ☐ Go for a swim
- ☐ Make S'mores
- ☐ Ride your bike on a trail
- ☐ Visit an old mining camp
- ☐ Zip line through the forest
- ☐ Find animal tracks and identify them
- ☐ Try out stand up paddle-boarding
- ☐ See a waterfall
- ☐ Walk under the bridge
- ☐ Collect leaves and identify them
- ☐ Camp and see the stars
- ☐ Count the animals you see